Books by Oxford Scientific Films

BEES AND HONEY
Photographs by David Thompson

THE BUTTERFLY CYCLE
Photographs by Dr. John Cooke

HOUSE MOUSE
Photographs by David Thompson

THE SPIDER'S WEB
Photographs by Dr. John Cooke

THE STICKLEBACK CYCLE
Photographs by David Thompson

COMMON FROG
Photographs by George Bernard

The Chicken and the Egg

By Oxford Scientific Films

Photographs by George Bernard and Peter Parks

G. P. Putnam's Sons   New York

First American Edition 1979
Text / Nature's Way Copyright © 1979 by G. Whizzard Publications Ltd.
Photographs © 1979 by Oxford Scientific Films Ltd.
All rights reserved.
Printed by New Interlitho (S.p.a.)

Library of Congress Cataloging in Publication Data
Main entry under title: The chicken and the egg
SUMMARY: Text and photos focus on the behavior, pecking order,
and egg production of the most numerous species of bird.
I. Chickens — Juvenile literature. [I. Chickens — Habits and behavior]
I. Bernard, George 1949- II. Parks, Peter, 1942- III. Oxford Scientific Films.
SF487.5.C44 1979   636.5   78-23663
ISBN 0-399 20676-0

The Chicken and the Egg

The domestic chicken or fowl (*Gallus domesticus*) is the most numerous species of bird on earth. More than eight million of them are hatched every year. These birds are descendants of the jungle fowl (*Gallus gallus*), which still lives wild in parts of Southeast Asia. Centuries of domestication and selective breeding have produced hundreds of different varieties of chicken, but whatever their color, shape or size, they all share the same basic characteristics.

Chickens are bred for their meat and eggs, increasingly under the artificial conditions of "intensive production systems." The birds are crammed into wire cages, fed a restricted diet and frequently have their beaks removed so that they can't peck each other. It is a cruel and unnatural existence. Still, there are plenty of the traditional farmyard chickens to be found, although they are much less common now than they were fifteen or twenty years ago. In these more sympathetic surroundings the birds are better able to develop their natural habits.

Live insects, grubs and worms, seeds and young green shoots, are the favorite natural food of chickens. They find these morsels by busily pecking away in the grass and soil with their sharp beaks, using their large feet and claws to scratch up the surface of the ground. Chickens also eat a lot of grit. The hard, flinty kind aids their digestion. The soft, chalky variety is full of the calcium needed for bone formation and, in the case of hens, to form eggshells. Water, too, is an important part of the daily diet.

The food that the chicken eats is not digested immediately, but is stored in a small sac under its neck called the crop. From there it travels to the stomach and gizzard (a sort of second stomach), where the hard pieces of food are crushed and ground by strong muscles, using the insoluble grit as a grinding "tool."

In a mixed flock of chickens one bird is always more dominant than the others. Usually it is a cockerel (male), but it can be a hen (female). The dominant bird will peck the others out of the way to get at the best food and sleeping place, and in general rules the roost. In fact, a chain of authority is established throughout the flock, with each bird subservient to the next, right down the line. This is known as the "pecking order."

Much of a chicken's day is spent searching for food, but it does stop from time to time to preen and take dust baths. Preening is stroking the feathers with the beak to clean and oil them. The chicken collects the oil on its beak from the preen gland, which is situated at the base of the tail.

Dust bathing consists of finding or scratching out a dry hole in the ground, squatting into it and fluffing dust into the feathers. Exactly why chickens have dust baths is not known — few other birds practice the habit — but it is thought to be connected with cleaning the smaller feathers and keeping them free of parasites. Both preening and dust bathing are obvious forms of relaxation and usually take place when the birds are feeling sleepy or well fed.

Most chickens can fly (if they haven't had their wings clipped), although not powerfully or far. If there isn't a hen house (and sometimes even if there is), they like to perch during the day and roost at night in the branches of trees that provide some shelter. Cockerels awake at the first light of dawn and begin to crow, making sure that nothing within earshot sleeps late.

A very recognizable feature of the cockerel is the long, sharp spur on the back of each leg. The bird uses these when fighting or defending itself, jumping up and kicking out at its opponent. Hens also have spurs, but they are much smaller and not used for anything.

The most common predators of chickens, apart from humans, are foxes and, for young birds and eggs, rats. Both predators strike mainly at night. Sometimes chickens, particularly cockerels, fight back, but usually the animal has its way and dozens of birds may be destroyed in a single fox attack.

The natural season for the chicken to start laying its eggs is toward the end of winter, when the days begin to lengthen. The hen, or pullet (the name for the female during its first year of egg laying), only needs to be mated with a cockerel if the intention is to breed and produce chicks. In the absence of a male, only unfertilized eggs are laid. Some people claim to be able to tell a slight difference in taste between fertilized and unfertilized eggs, but there is no scientific explanation for this. The only visual clue is a tiny white speck on the edge of the yolk, which is the early beginning of the chick embryo.

One male to every twelve females is a good ratio for breeding. In a farmyard a cockerel is likely to mate with a hen or pullet every two or three days.

although once a week is sufficient for a steady supply of fertile eggs. When mating, the male mounts the squatting female from behind and crouches on her back, balancing with partly outstretched wings. He rubs his vent, the large opening below the bird's tail, against hers for a few moments, stimulating it until his sperm is ejected. The sperm travels up the female's passage, or oviduct, and fertilizes her.

A normal healthy farmyard hen will lay about 180 to 200 eggs a year. Some lay a few more, many less. It greatly depends on conditions, such as how the birds are cared for, their feed, and so on. The figure is the same whether the eggs are fertilized or unfertilized. A hen usually lays no more than one egg a day.

Most chicken eggs have either white or brown shells (some hens in South America lay blue-shelled eggs), but whatever the color the food value is the same. Half of the yolk consists of fats and proteins, providing the main sustenance for the growing chick embryo. The white, or albumen, is 90 percent water, with additional protein. Eggs also contain iron, calcium and a variety of vitamins, which is why they are so nutritious.

The egg yolk develops in the ovary of the hen, and the white and shell are added gradually as the egg passes down the oviduct. The egg eventually emerges from the vent. If allowed to, a hen will lay her eggs almost anywhere — in a hedge, haystack, even among a pile of old clothes — as long as the place is sheltered and reasonably warm.

The hen waits until she has a clutch of about six to ten eggs (up to twelve days) before she begins to brood, or sit on them. Once the incubation starts, however, the hen rarely leaves the eggs for more than an hour at a time so that they won't get cold.

The chick embryo develops quickly inside the egg. Within a few days the head, body and tail have begun to take shape. By the end of the second week the feathers are well formed. Several days before hatching the chick may be heard cheeping, with the hen clucking in reply. Each recognizes the other's call, thus helping to reduce the risk of confusion with any other family nearby.

After three weeks' incubation the chick is ready to emerge. It jabs at the underside of the shell with a special egg tooth on its beak, working its way around the middle of the egg. This process is known as "pipping," and can take anywhere from twenty minutes to fourteen hours to complete. When ready, the chick pushes the two halves of the shell apart and comes out into the open. The eggs tend to hatch within a few hours of each other even though they may have been laid several days apart. The egg tooth falls off within twenty-four hours.

The new chicks are tired, weak and wet, and can lose heat rapidly. For the next few days the hen will keep them covered for much of the time. Drying out takes up to three hours. During this time the chick exercises, gains balance control, sleeps, stands and lies down, all the while making cheeping sounds.

For the first day after hatching the chick relies on yolk reserves within its body for food. On the second or third day it starts to feed and drink, taking its example from the hen. With its down feathers now dry, fluffed and acting as a good insulator, the chick generates its own body heat — although for a while yet it will need additional warmth from the hen.

Hens (or pullets) start laying eggs when they are about twenty weeks old. Their peak laying period is the spring and early summer. With the approach of autumn the birds begin to lose their feathers, or molt. The shorter days are a sign that the laying season is drawing to a close, and most of them stop producing eggs. Some birds start laying again as soon as the molt is over, usually eight to ten weeks later. Others remain inactive until the late winter.

A chicken can live as long as twelve years, but the demands of the dinner table seldom allow it to. It is usually a case of first the egg, then the chicken.

These chickens live in the farmyard.

Head of a cockerel (male)  and a hen (female).

Chickens scratch up the ground with their long claws and peck away in search of grit,

insects, grubs, seeds and young green shoots.

Each bird has its place in the "pecking order"

with the stronger ones dominating the others.

These chickens are preening their feathers

and having a dust bath.

Cockerels crow at dawn — and make sure that nothing sleeps late.

They use the sharp spur on the back of each leg when fighting.

When mating the cockerel mounts the hen from behind.

Hens will lay their eggs almost anywhere

but usually in a coop or hen house.

The eggs come out of the large opening below the hen's tail.

The hen sits on the eggs when she has laid from six to ten eggs.

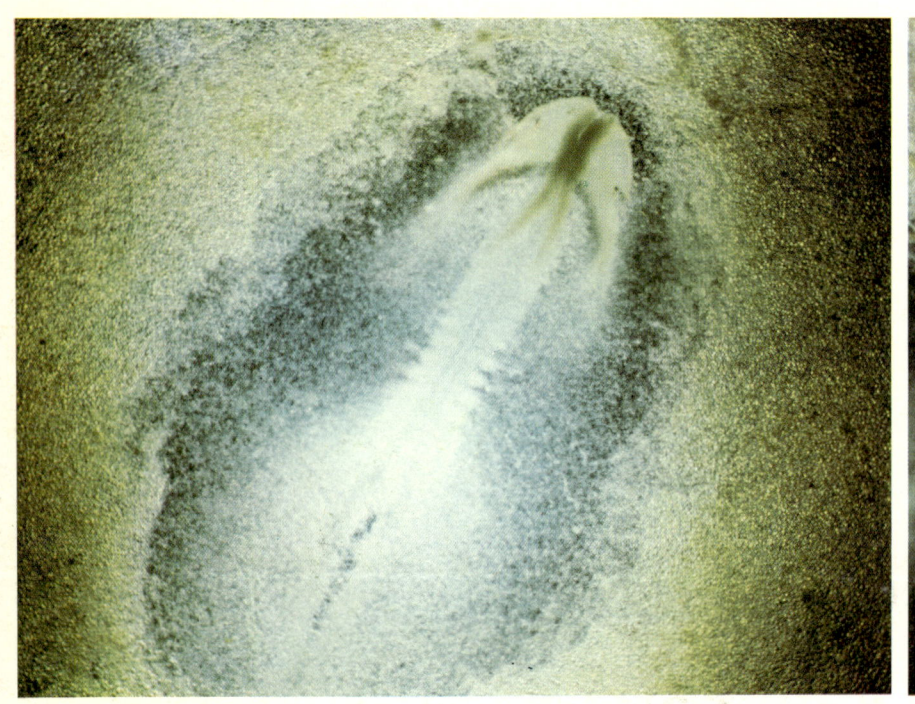 

after twenty hours after forty-five hours

The beginning of a chick embryo growing inside the egg.

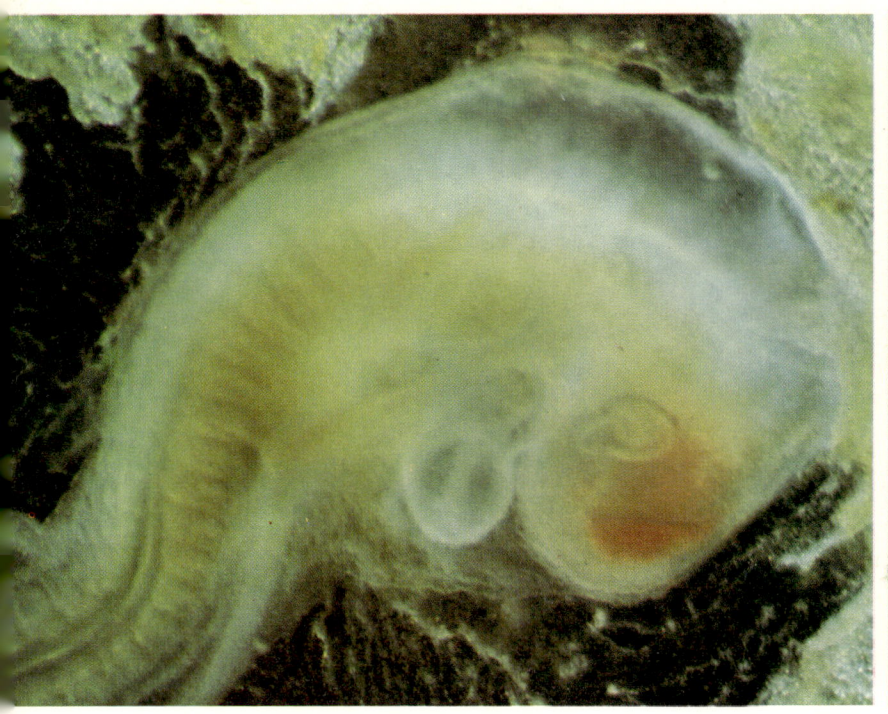

At two and a half days the head, body and tail are well developed.

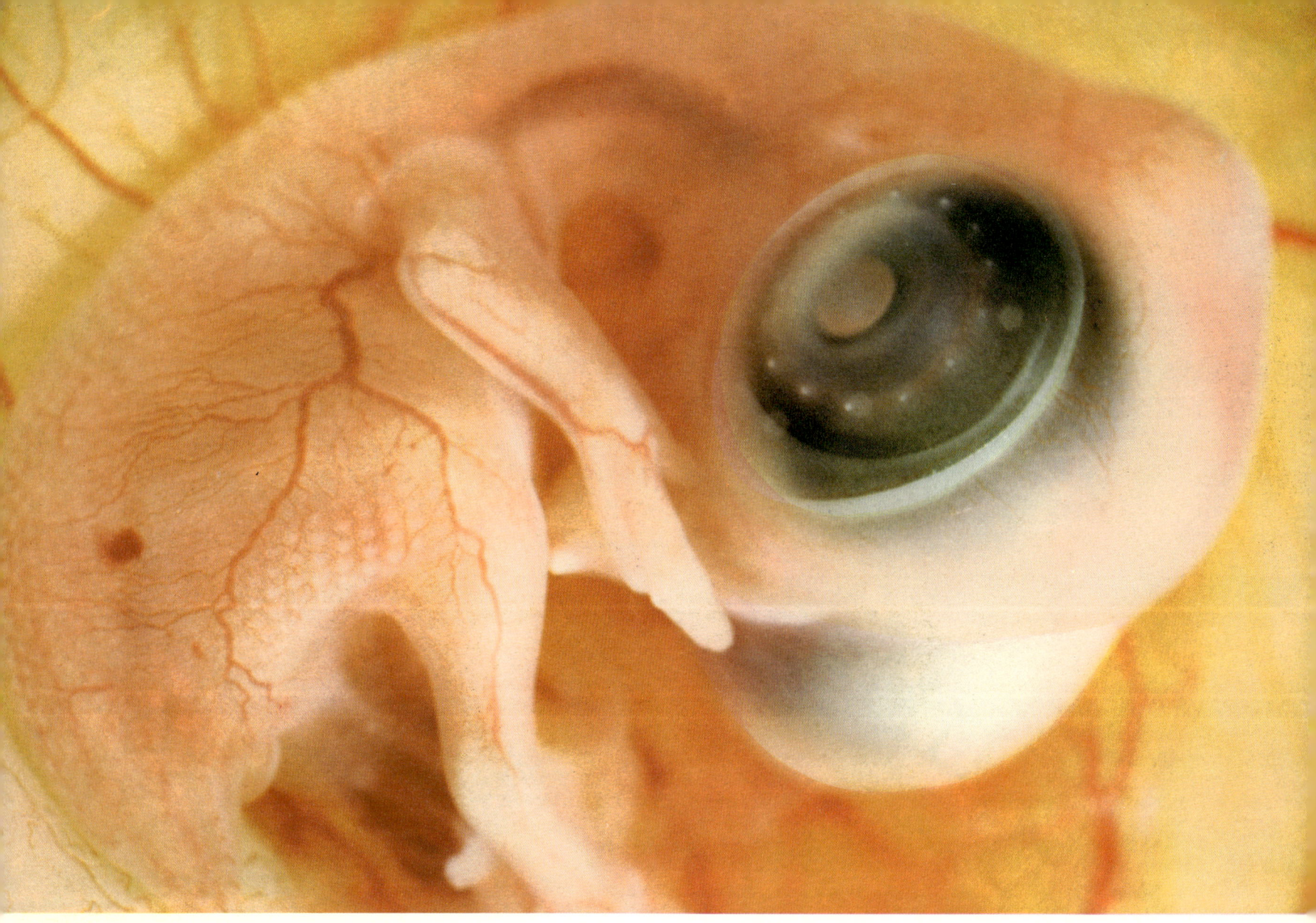
After six days the eyes can be clearly seen and the embryo is covered with skin.

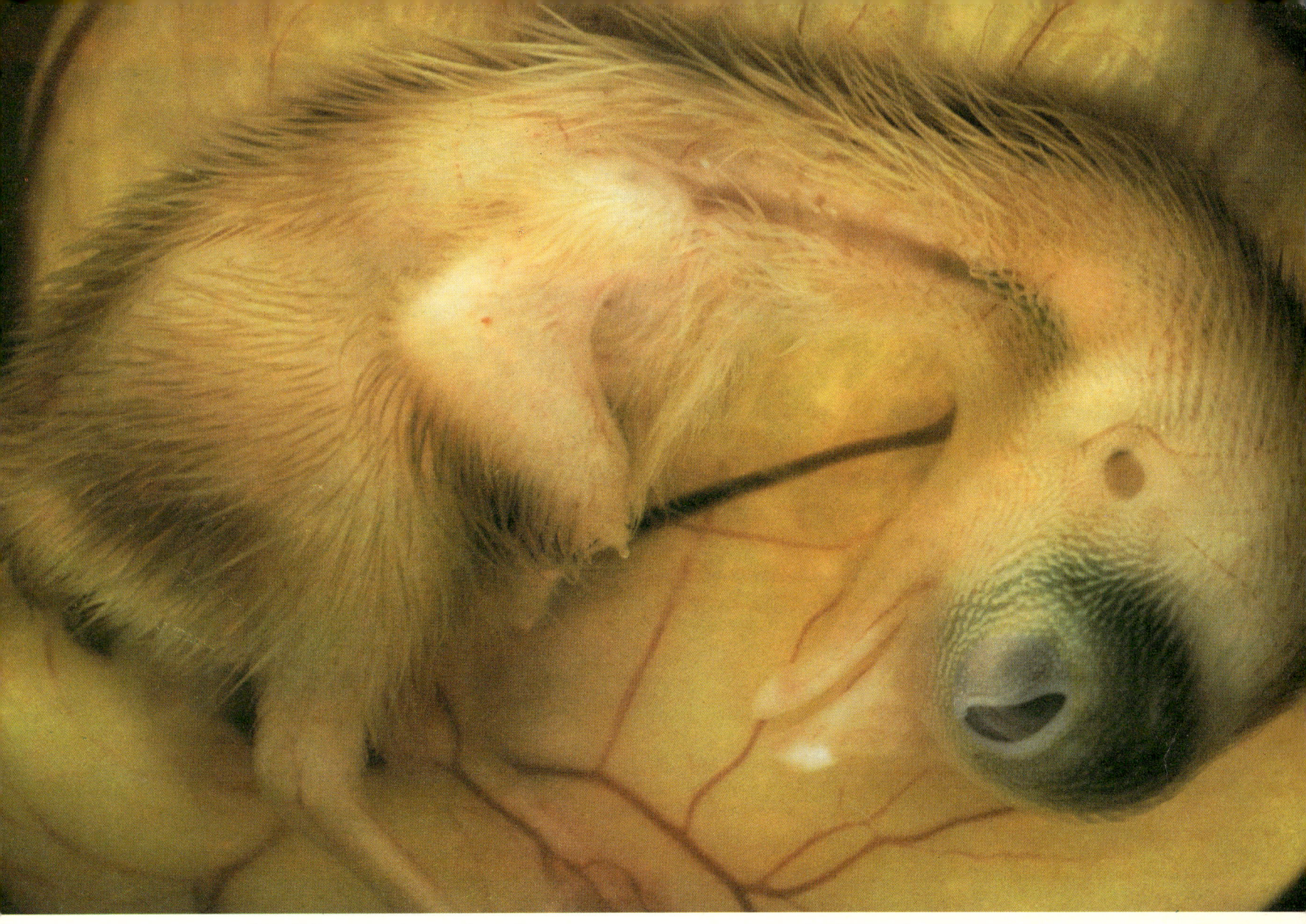

At fifteen days feathers are growing and the white egg tooth has appeared on the end of the beak.

After nearly three weeks the chick is ready to hatch.

It breaks through the shell with its egg tooth and comes out into the open.

The new chick is tired, weak and wet and has to be kept warm by the hen for a few days.

These young hens are a few weeks old. After twenty weeks or so they start laying eggs.